Putting It All Together

Putting It All Together

Readings for Students of English as a Second Language

George M. Jacobs
and
Michael A. Power

Ann Arbor
The University of Michigan Press

To Fong and Kikuyo

Copyright © by the University of Michigan 1991
All rights reserved
ISBN 0-472-08158-6
Library of Congress Catalog Card No. 91-67105
Published in the United States of America by
The University of Michigan Press
Manufactured in the United States of America
1994 1993 1992 1991   4 3 2 1

Contents

Teacher's Introduction vii

Suggestions to the Student xi

Map of Cities and Countries xiii

Chapter 1
Going to School in Other Countries 1
   Strategy: Looking Ahead to Learn about Unknown Words

Chapter 2
How Long Will You Live? 9
   Strategy: Connecting Ideas Using Also, For example, *and* Therefore

Chapter 3
From the Village to the City 17
   Strategy: Looking for Words That Mean the Same or Are Opposites

Chapter 4
A New Future 23
   Strategy: Using "Wh" Words

Chapter 5
Guns, Guns, Too Many Guns? 29
   Strategy: Finding the Same Word in Another Context

Chapter 6
Two Kinds of Medicine 35
   Strategy: Using Possessive Pronouns

Chapter 7
Learning about Other Countries without Leaving Home 43
   Strategy: Connecting Ideas Using And *and* But

Chapter 8
Is There Enough Food in the World for Everyone? 49
   Strategy: Getting Help from Other Paragraphs

Chapter 9
Two Friends with Different Futures 57
Strategy: Using Infinitives

Chapter 10
Clean Water and the Women of Burkina Faso 65
Strategy: Connecting Ideas Using Additionally, Although, *and* Because

Chapter 11
Can the Rain Forest Be Saved? 73
Strategy: Linking Cause and Effect

Chapter 12
Are Languages Alive? 79
Strategy: Using Words of Quantity

Chapter 13
Where Have All the Young People Gone? 87
Strategy: Using the Same Form of the Verb

Chapter 14
What Is the Definition of Peace? 93
Strategy: Using Context to Choose between Opposites

Answers to Comprehension Questions 101

Teacher's Introduction

The main goal of the readings in *Putting It All Together* is to develop the readers' skills in understanding written English through the use of context to guess the meaning of new, unknown words or to predict function words. We believe that reading is an *interactive* process. Readers not only *get* meaning from the text, they also *bring* meaning to the text, based on their experiences and expectations. Students of English as a second or foreign language may already be reading interactively in their native language, but they need specific practice to shift these skills to reading English. To help your students make this shift, we have designed the passages in *Putting It All Together* to call upon and develop specific strategies that skilled readers use.

In each passage the students will encounter many missing words. They will be given two or three words (or short phrases) to choose from to fill in the blank. Since all of these words are possibly correct, the students must use the context of the sentence and the passage as a whole to select the correct answer. The aim of these missing word exercises (also called *cloze* exercises) is to build higher level reading skills and to move students away from word-by-word reading to the more advanced skills of making inferences, generalizing, and synthesizing.

Suggestions for the Teacher

Prereading

Each chapter begins with a suggested activity entitled Before You Read. These activities promote interaction and prepare students to better comprehend and enjoy the readings. Other prereading activities can be added as you wish, but we suggest that you incorporate *some* prereading into each chapter.

Previewing/Skimming

The Prereading Checklist before each passage is designed to encourage students to use the strategy of *previewing* by having them skim through the whole passage before starting on the missing words. This is also why we have put the word choices on a separate page: to discourage premature guessing. After previewing, you could follow up with whole-class or group discussions of what the passage might be about, based on the clues students picked up while skimming.

Using the Whole Context

Tell students to read the whole passage before trying to fill in any of the blanks. This will give them a more complete idea of what is happening in the reading. Also, when they start to fill in the blanks, they should be reminded that the necessary context clues are not always *before* the blank; sometimes they come *after* the blank, sometimes even in the next paragraph.

Feedback

Besides finding the correct word, it is important for students to understand the clues they used to make that choice. Discussion with the whole class or in groups will enable them to refine their strategies. Schedule a feedback session at the end of each lesson to summarize what was learned and what strategies were practiced.

Questions

The questions after each passage are written to help students progress from comprehension—finding specific facts—to discussing the issues raised in the text. These passages were written to stimulate thought and interactive discussion of topics of interest and concern to anyone learning about new languages and cultures. You may want to add questions of your own or ask students to write their own questions. You can also add activities related to the topics, such as writing on related themes, making maps and displays, sharing related experiences, predicting what will happen, and comparing and contrasting the cultural aspects of the issues.

Using AV Equipment

Putting the cloze passage on an overhead projector can make it easier for you and your students to show the clues in the passage that lead to the correct word choice.

Developing Strategies

Although you can identify others as well, it will be helpful to introduce or review one or two reading strategies with your students before each reading. (Some of these are included in the text as Warm-Up exercises.) As you go through the examples in the Warm-Up, you may want to ask students to create further examples. The best choice for each example is explained.

Group Work

These passages are exercises for developing reading skill and are not designed as tests. We suggest that students work as cooperatively as possible, getting help from you, each other, the dictionary, and all of the other resources that skilled readers use.

One idea would be to have students work in groups of two to four. After reading the whole passage once silently, they can work on the missing words together, sharing their guesses and explaining their strategies. In working on the comprehension and discussion questions, you can have one student in each group read the questions, and together they could discuss possible answers. Such activities encourage students to work together and allow them to learn from each other's strategies, ideas, and experiences.

Suggestions to the Student

When you are reading in English, you often see words that you don't know. What do you do then? Using the dictionary is one good idea, but there are many other things you can do to help you understand what you read. In this book you will practice many skills for becoming a better reader of English.

One important skill is using the context to understand words and ideas. *Context* is the information in the rest of the passage. Guessing means looking at the passage and trying to think about the meaning. You should look for hints in the rest of the passage to help you understand; don't look at just the word or sentence which you don't understand. Your teacher will help you look for hints.

The readings in this book are like puzzles. When you look at the passage you will see that some words are missing. To solve the puzzle you have to choose the best word or words to complete each sentence. Most of the missing words will be words you have already studied. Think about your reasons for choosing each answer and try to explain your reasons to your classmates or the teacher.

Here is an example.

Tom eats _____ orange every day.

a   two   an

The correct choice is *an*. Write it in the blank space. Why should you choose *an*? Because *orange* begins with the vowel *o,* and there is only one orange.

As you finish each reading, you will find that there are also some questions for you to answer. Think about what information in the passage helped you find the answers, and discuss the topics with your classmates and the teacher.

Cities
(indicated by a ● on the map)

K   Kobe, Japan
S   Sweetwater, Tennessee, U.S.A.
J   Juneau, Alaska, U.S.A.
S   Shanghai, China
Y   York, England
F   Fairbanks, Alaska, U.S.A.
N   New York, New York, U.S.A.
M   Mexico City, Mexico

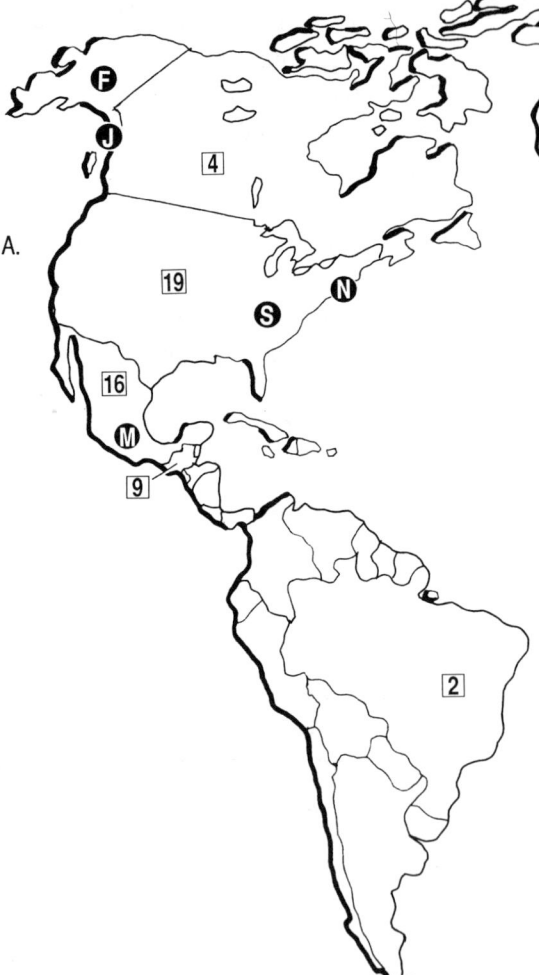

Countries
(indicated by a ☐ on the map)

1   American Samoa
2   Brazil
3   Burkina Faso
4   Canada
5   (The People's Republic of) China
6   England
7   France
8   Germany
9   Guatemala
10 India
11 Israel
12 Italy
13 Japan
14 Kenya
15 Laos
16 Mexico
17 New Zealand
18 South Africa
19 United States of America

Map of Cities and Countries

Chapter 1
Going To School in Other Countries

Before You Read

There are many reasons why people study. Why do you study English? Below is a list of reasons why some people study English. How important are these reasons to you? If a reason is *very important* to you, write VI next to the reason. If a reason is only *slightly important* to you, write SI next to it. If a reason is *not important* to you, write NI next to it.

I study English to

____ get a good job.

____ make my parents happy.

____ learn about the culture of English-speaking countries.

____ prepare to use English to study other subjects.

____ prepare to live in an English-speaking country.

____ understand English movies, television, and music.

_____ have friends who speak English.

_____ take vacations in English-speaking countries.

_____ other (Write a reason that is not on this list.)

Prereading Checklist

Before you start reading the passage "Going to School in Other Countries," skim it quickly looking for words you think might be important. Think about the illustration and the title. Try to get a general idea of what the passage is about.

Now try to answer these questions. Discuss your answers with your classmates. You might have different answers, but that is all right. Sometimes there are no right or wrong answers. Thinking about these questions will help prepare you to understand and enjoy what you read.

- Does this passage mainly tell a story or does it give information?
- Is the passage about the present, the past, or the future? Or is it a combination?
- Are there people in the passage? If so, what are their names, or what else can you find out about them?
- What are some words in the passage that seem to be important?
- After you discuss your answers, think about the illustration and the title again. Now, what do you think the passage is about? What do you already know about this topic?

Warm-Up

Strategy: Looking Ahead to Learn about Unknown Words
When we see a word that we do not know, there are many places to look for information about the word. One place to look is at the words that come after the unknown word. Sometimes there will be information later in the same sentence, the same paragraph, or even farther into the reading passage. This information may help us understand the unknown word.

Example A

_____ is the country with the largest population in Central America.

Israel   Guatemala   Kenya

Guatemala is the correct choice. When we look ahead, we see that the word we need is the name of a country in Central America. Guatemala is the only choice that is a country in Central America.

Example B

My favorite sport is _____ . I enjoy trying to kick the ball into the net.

football/soccer   swimming   ping-pong

Football is the correct choice. In some countries, people call it soccer. When we look ahead, we read that in this sport the ball is kicked into a net. There is no ball or net in swimming, and we do not kick the ball in ping-pong. Therefore football (or soccer) is the correct choice.

Going to School in Other Countries

This reading is about the schools people go to when they live in other countries. First try to read and understand as much of the story as you can. Then look at the Word Choices section and try to guess the missing words. Finally, you can look at the vocabulary list for help with words you don't know.

In the _____ (1) town of Sweetwater, Tennessee, there is a place where children _____ (2) called Meiji Gakuin. That doesn't sound like the name of an American school, does it? In fact, it is a Japanese school, and all of the students in that school are the _____ (3) and sons of Japanese employees of a Japanese company in Sweetwater. In Kobe, Japan, there is a school called the _____ (4) Academy. This school has this name because it was started by people from Canada. Not all of the students there are Canadians, but almost none of the students are Japanese. They are the children of foreigners who live in Japan.

All over the world there are schools for people who come from other countries and want their _____ (5) to study in schools that are the same as the schools they have at home. Often, these people live in communities in which everybody is a _____ (6), and therefore, they have little contact with the local people.

For example, in _____ (7), China before World War II, there was a separate city within Shanghai where _____ (8) foreigners could live. All Chinese had to leave this section of the _____ (9) before night time. The children who lived in this section of Shanghai went to American, French, German, or other non-Chinese schools.

Some people believe that it is important for children living abroad to study in their own language and to learn the same things that children in their home country are learning. For example, they believe that _____ (10) children living in Brazil should go to schools that use the Italian language and teach the same things that they teach in schools in Italy. This _____ (11) the students when they go back home.

_____ (12), other people disagree. They believe that children _____ (13) a lot of valuable information by going to the regular school in the country where they live. Children can learn a new language, and they can learn a new culture. The schools in another country may be _____ (14) the schools in the home country, but learning about another country and sharing the lives of the people of the new country are important. Living abroad should be more than _____ (15) foreign food and seeing new buildings.

Going to School in Other Countries

Word Choices

1. U.S., Japanese, Chinese
2. swim, sleep, study
3. companies, employees, daughters
4. Canadian, American, Japanese
5. parents, friends, children
6. student, movie star, foreigner
7. Shanghai, Beijing, Kuala Lumpur
8. only, no, all
9. school, city, hospital
10. Italian, Brazilian, Japanese
11. will help, helped, did help
12. Also, Therefore, However
13. learn, eat, wear
14. the same as, different from, better than
15. watching, eating, listening to

Vocabulary

abroad—in another country
disagree—have a different idea
employees—workers
foreigners—people from another country
section—part
separate—different
Tennessee—a state in the United States
valuable—important

Comprehension Questions

1. In what country is the Meiji Gakuin school?
2. Where is the Canadian Academy?
3. Before 1949, could Chinese people live anywhere in the city of Shanghai, China?
4. Why do some parents who live abroad send their children to special schools for foreign students?
5. Why do other parents who live abroad send their children to the same school where the local children study?

Questions for Discussion

1. In your country, are there special schools for the children of foreigners?
2. Why do people who live abroad often like to live with people from their own country?
3. Is it useful for children living abroad to learn the language of their new country? Please explain your answer.
4. What does this sentence mean? "Living abroad should be more than eating foreign food and seeing new buildings." What does this mean to a foreigner who is living in *your* country?
5. In what kind of school do you think children should study when they live abroad? Please explain your answer.
6. What about foreigners in your country? Do they like to learn about your country's culture? Do they like to have many friends from your country?

Word Choices: Correct Answers

1. U.S. (or American) (The town has an American name.)
2. study (The main thing you do in a school is study.)
3. daughters (It matches "sons.")
4. Canadian (The next sentence mentions Canada.)
5. children
6. foreigner (It says they have little contact with *local* people.)
7. Shanghai (The clue is later in the sentence.)
8. only (The Chinese had to leave.)
9. city (Look in the sentence before this one.)
10. Italian (The clue is later in the sentence.)
11. will help ("When they go back home" tells you it is in the future.)
12. However (*Disagree* shows contrast.)
13. learn (We *learn* information.)
14. different from (The rest of the sentence after "but" shows contrast.)
15. eating (It is more fun to eat food than to watch food or listen to it!)

Chapter 2
How Long Will You Live?

Before You Read

Do you know how old your family members are? Make a list of their names and ages.

Do you know any people who are very old? What do you know about them? Are they healthy? What do they do every day?

How did they live so long? For example, some people say that regular exercise helped them live a long time. What do older people in your country do after they stop working?

Prereading Checklist

Before you start reading the passage "How Long Will You Live?" skim it quickly looking for words you think might be important. Think about the illustration and the title. Try to get a general idea of what the passage is about.

Now try to answer these questions. Discuss your answers with your classmates. Thinking about these questions will help prepare you to understand and enjoy what you read.

10 / How Long Will You Live?

- Does this passage mainly tell a story or does it give information?
- Is the passage about the present, the past, or the future? Or is it a combination?
- Are there people in the passage? If so, what are their names, or what else can you find out about them?
- What are some words in the passage that seem to be important?
- After you discuss your answers, think about the illustration and the title again. Now, what do you think the passage is about? What do you already know about this topic?

Warm-Up

Strategy: Connecting Ideas Using *Also*, *For example*, and *Therefore*

Also, for example, and *therefore* are words that connect sentences and ideas together. But each of these connectors has a different meaning.

Also is used to add an idea that is similar to an idea already in the reading passage. *For example* is used to give an example of an idea already in the passage. *Therefore* shows that one thing is the result of another. Let's look at three examples.

Example A

In Thailand, farmers grow a lot of rice. _____ , farmers in Thailand grow a large amount of fruit.

Also For example Therefore

Also is the correct choice because the first sentence tells us that farmers in Thailand grow rice, and the second sentence *adds* that they grow fruit.

Example B

In Thailand, farmers grow a lot of rice. _____ , in 1987 they grew 450 million tons of rice.

Also For example Therefore

For example is the correct choice because the second sentence gives an *example* of how much rice is grown.

Example C

In Thailand, farmers grow a lot of rice. _____ , Thailand can sell rice to other countries.

Also   For example   Therefore

Therefore is the correct choice because the second sentence shows the result of the first sentence: Thailand can sell rice to other countries because its farmers grow a lot of rice.

How Long Will You Live?

People are living longer today than they used to. This reading passage talks about why people live longer. It also talks about some of the problems that older people have. First try to read and understand as much of the story as you can. Then look at the Word Choices section and try to guess the missing words. Finally, you can look at the vocabulary list for help with words you don't know.

Thousands of years ago, people did not live a long time. The average person only lived to be twenty-five or thirty years old. Twenty percent of the babies died before they were twelve months old, and another thirty percent did not live to be five years old. All together, _____ (1) percent of the people died before their fifth birthday.

Today, people live a much _____ (2) time. One reason people live longer is that the water we drink is cleaner. Clean water does not carry diseases. _____ (3), medicine is better today.

In some countries the average person lives to be seventy or older. There are many people _____ (4) live to be eighty, ninety, and even one hundred. Therefore, we see more and more _____ (5) people. Many people can know their _____ (6) and their great grandparents.

Often women live longer than men. _____ (7), in Japan, on the average, women will live to be eighty-five, but men will only live to be eighty. _____ (8), many Japanese husbands will die before their wives.

In the future, people probably _____ (9) live longer than today. There are many things we can do to help people live longer. _____ (10), we can see that everyone has enough medicine to fight disease. _____ (11), everyone needs to have enough to eat. Today, many people die or are sick because they do not have enough food. Another way to make life longer is to _____ (12) wars. Every year thousands of people are killed in wars.

Yes, people live longer today, but some young people say they do not want to live to be old. They have three reasons for this opinion. _____ (13), they say that older people are always sick. Second, they say that old people are _____ (14) because they do not have jobs. Third, they say everyone forgets old people. _____ (15), old people are lonely.

Word Choices

1. five, thirty, fifty
2. shorter, older, longer
3. Also, For example, Therefore
4. where, what, who
5. older, taller, younger
6. children, grandparents, teachers
7. Also, For Example, Therefore
8. Also, For Example, Therefore
9. did, do, will
10. Also, For example, Therefore
11. Also, For example, Therefore
12. begin, end, start
13. Also, First, Therefore
14. rich, poor, happy
15. Also, For example, Therefore

Vocabulary

average—usual, common
disease—sickness, something wrong with your body
great grandparents—the parents of your grandparents
lonely—sad because you are alone
medicine—something you eat or drink when you are sick
opinion—belief, idea

Comprehension Questions

1. Do people live longer today, or did people live longer thousands of years ago?
2. Thousands of years ago, what percent of the babies lived to be older than one year old?
3. A widow is a woman whose husband has died. A widower is a man whose wife has died. In Japan are there more widows or more widowers?
4. How many people die each year in wars?
5. Why do people live longer today?

Questions for Discussion

1. Are your grandparents or great-grandparents alive? If not, how old were they when they died?
2. What can we do to help ourselves live longer?
3. What can people who are not poor do to help poor people live longer?
4. How old do you think you will live to be? Close your eyes and imagine that you are eighty-five years old. How do you feel? Where do you live? Who do you live with? What do you do every day?
5. What is your opinion about being old? Do you want to be old?
6. Is it possible to live *too* long? Do you think people who are over eighty years old can be happy? Explain your answer.

Word Choices: Correct Answers

1. fifty
2. longer
3. Also (The medicine is better, *and* the water is cleaner.)
4. who
5. older
6. grandparents
7. For example (Japan is an *example* of a country where women live longer than men.)
8. Therefore (This is the *result* of Japanese women living to be eighty-five while Japanese men die at eighty, on the average.)
9. will
10. For example (This sentence gives an *example* of what we can do to help people live longer.)
11. Also (This sentence *adds* another example of what we can do to help people live longer.)
12. end
13. First
14. poor
15. Therefore ("Old people are lonely" is the *result* of "everyone forgets old people.")

Chapter 3
From the Village to the City

Before You Read

Interview two of your classmates. Ask them if they would like to live in a city or in a small town. Ask why. Tell them where *you* would like to live, and why. Do the students in your class who come from small towns want to live in a small town? How about students from cities?

Prereading Checklist

Before you start reading the passage "From the Village to the City," try to skim it quickly looking for words you think might be important. Think about the illustration and the title. Try to get a general idea of what the passage is about.
    Now try to answer these questions. Discuss your answers with your classmates. Thinking about these questions will help prepare you to understand and enjoy what you read.

- Does this passage mainly tell a story or does it give information?
- Is the passage about the present, the past, or the future? Or is it a combination?

18 / From the Village to the City

- Are there people in the passage? If so, what are their names, or what else can you find out about them?
- What are some words in the passage that seem to be important?
- After you discuss your answers, think about the illustration and the title again. Now, what do you think the passage is about? What do you already know about this topic?

Warm-Up

Strategy: Looking for Words That Mean the Same or Are Opposites

One way to guess which word goes in a blank is to look for words that mean the same or the opposite of other words in the reading passage. Let's look at two examples.

Example A

A desert is very dry, but a jungle is very _____ .

hot   important   wet

Wet is the correct choice because it's the opposite of *dry*. (*But* is a clue to look for an opposite.)

Example B

Gisela is happy because she got an A in English. Her parents are also _____ about her grade.

angry   glad   teachers

Glad is the correct choice because it means the same as *happy*. (*Also* is a clue to look for a word that has the same meaning.)

There will not always be words like *but* and *also* to tell us which word to choose, but if we understand the meaning of the passage, we can decide if the correct word for the blank will be the opposite of or mean the same as another word in the passage.

From the Village to the City

This reading is about changes in the places where people live. First, try to read and understand as much of the passage as you can. Then look at the Word Choices section and try to guess the missing words. Finally, you can look at the vocabulary list for help with words you don't know.

Maria Sandoval and her mother live in Mexico City, the capital of Mexico, and one of the largest cities in the world. Maria asked her mother, "When did you come to Mexico City?" Her mother answered that she came in 1930, but that many things are _____ (1) now. Today, many _____ (2) people live in Mexico City. There are crowds everywhere, on the streets, in the stores, and on the buses.

Maria asked, " _____ (3) the people the same today?" Her mother said, "I don't know. I think people are not very friendly today. People are in a hurry. They _____ (4) everywhere they go. No one has time to talk." Maria wondered why so many people _____ (5) the city. Mrs. Sandoval said, "They come for the same reason your _____ (6) and I came in 1930. They want jobs, _____ (7) they want electricity, public transportation, and other features of modern life."

Maria thought about that. Then she asked, "Are you glad that you are here, _____ (8) do you want to return to the little village where you were born?" Her mother said that sometimes she wished she was in the village again. It is _____ (9) there because there is no city noise. And, people are friendlier. They have time to _____ (10). She said that also she would like to see all the green trees in the village. In the city there are _____ (11) trees. "But, Maria, the answer to your _____ (12) is that I am glad I live in the city. _____ (13) we have jobs and a more comfortable life."

Maria said, "Someday I want to see the village where you were born." Mrs. Sandoval smiled and said, "Yes, maybe _____ (14) Christmas we can go there together. But now you are busy with your job. I hope the village is the same but I don't know. _____ (15) changes."

Word Choices

1. different, the same, smaller
2. happier, more, fewer
3. Were, Are, Was
4. walk, talk, run
5. come to, leave, talk to
6. grandparents, children, wife
7. but, however, and
8. or, and, therefore
9. noisy, quiet, dangerous
10. run, work, talk
11. a lot of, beautiful, few
12. reason, city, question
13. There, Here, But
14. December, next, last
15. Everything, Nothing, Villages

Vocabulary

crowds—large groups of people
transportation—buses, cars, trains, etc.
village—a very small town

Comprehension Questions

1. Is Mexico City today the same as or different from the way it was in 1930? Please explain.
2. Why do people come to Mexico City?
3. Was Maria born in a village or in Mexico City?
4. Was Maria's mother born in a village or in a city?
5. Does Mrs. Sandoval want to live in a village or in a city?

Questions for Discussion

1. How is a village better than a city?
2. How is a city better than a village?
3. Has the place where *you* live changed? If it has, how has it changed?

4. Do you want to live in a village or in a city? Why?
5. How can we make cities friendlier, quieter, and greener?

Word Choices: Correct Answers

1. different (*Different* is the opposite of *same*.)
2. more
3. Are
4. run (*Run* has a meaning similar to *in a hurry*.)
5. come to
6. grandparents
7. and
8. or
9. quiet (*Quiet* is almost the opposite of *noise*.)
10. talk
11. few (*Few* is almost the opposite of *all*.)
12. question (Mrs. Sandoval *answers* Maria's question.)
13. Here
14. next
15. Everything

Chapter 4
A New Future

Before You Read

The title of this passage is "A New Future." What does that make you think of? Draw a picture to show one idea of the future. Think about your picture. Does it show a happy future or a sad future? How is your picture different from life today? Show your picture to the class and explain your ideas.

Prereading Checklist

Before you start reading the passage "A New Future," skim it quickly looking for words you think might be important. Think about the illustration and the title. Try to get a general idea of what the passage is about.
   Now try to answer these questions. Discuss your answers with your classmates. Thinking about these questions will help prepare you to understand and enjoy what you read.

- Does this passage mainly tell a story or does it give information?
- Is the passage about the present, the past, or the future? Or is it a combination?

- Are there people in the passage? If so, what are their names, or what else can you find out about them?
- What are some words in the passage that seem to be important?
- After you discuss your answers, think about the illustration and the title again. Now, what do you think the passage is about? What do you already know about this topic?

Warm-Up

Strategy: Using "Wh" Words

"Wh" words include *when, where, which, who,* and *why*. We usually think that "wh" words are for questions: for example, "Where are my shoes?" But we can also use "wh" words in other kinds of sentences.

When tells about time. *Where* tells about place. *Which* means there are different possibilities. *Who* tells about people. *Why* is used with reasons. Let's look at three examples.

Example A

February 20th was the day _____ I got married.

when   who   why

When is the correct choice, because February 20th is a *time*.

Example B

Gail is the woman _____ married me.

when   who   why

Who is the correct choice, because *woman* refers to *people*.

Example C

He didn't ask his father _____ he was angry.

where   who   why

Why is the best choice because he didn't ask the *reason* his father was angry.

A New Future

This story is about some people in a fictional small town who had to make some hard decisions. First try to read and understand as much of the story as you can. Then look at the Word Choices section and try to guess the missing words. Finally, you can look at the vocabulary list for help with words you don't know.

"Time and tide wait for no man." Do you know _____ (1) quotation? Some people think it means that everything changes, and people cannot do anything about _____ (2). Do you agree? Read the following story before you answer the question.

One day a stranger came to the small village of Pomeray, _____ (3) there was a beautiful, wide river. He made an offer to the _____ (4). He said that he would like to build a factory in the village. He told them _____ (5) he wanted to build a factory there: the village was near a river of clean, cold water. He needed a lot of _____ (6) to keep the machines in his factory cool. At first, most of the people of the village were excited about the man's _____ (7). They _____ (8) that they would become rich and that they would have many modern conveniences.

However, some of the villagers had a _____ (9) idea. They told everybody what had happened in other towns _____ (10) factories were built. The people in these towns did not become rich. People _____ (11) knew how to run the machines came from other towns and took all of the good jobs in the factories. These new people also needed new homes, stores, and services. The towns grew much _____ (12) than the people expected, and they could not control the change.

After hearing these stories, the people of Pomeray decided to meet with the factory owner _____ (13). Together they made a plan for the future of the village. They thought of all of the things _____ (14) could change in their village, good and _____ (15). They made plans for all of these situations. First the people of _____ (16) and the factory owner agreed on a good plan, then they built the factory.

How do you think their plans worked out?

Word Choices

1. this, another, which
2. difference, change, effect
3. where, who, why
4. people, business, money
5. when, whom, why
6. money, time, water
7. famous, idea, machines
8. wondered, remembered, thought
9. different, new, worse
10. when, who, why
11. when, who, why
12. faster, over, better
13. alone, again, before
14. why, that, when
15. bad, important, wonderful
16. Pomeray, England, my town

Vocabulary

convenience—a useful or helpful machine, such as an electric oven
expect—to think something will happen
factory—a building where things are made
fictional—not true
make an offer—tell someone what you will do for them
quotation—something that was said by another person
run the machines—make the machines work
tide—the rise and fall of the ocean
worked out—resulted, ended

Comprehension Questions

1. Who came to the village of Pomeray?
2. At first, how did the people feel about the stranger's offer?
3. Did everyone agree with the stranger?
4. What happened to some other towns that built factories?
5. What did the people of Pomeray finally decide to do?

28 / A New Future

Questions for Discussion

1. What were the arguments for and against building the factory in Pomeray?
2. Why did the people of Pomeray change their minds about the factory?
3. Can you think of examples of real towns that had a problem like the one the people in this fictional town had? What happened?
4. Discuss some of the plans the people of Pomeray might have made to make the changes easier.
5. Is change always something that happens *to* us, or is it something we can control?

Word Choices: Correct Answers

1. this
2. change
3. where (The river was in Pomeray.)
4. people
5. why (The sentence needs a word that refers to *the reason*.)
6. water
7. idea
8. thought
9. different
10. when (They told about the time the factories were built.)
11. who (The sentence needs a word that refers to *people*.)
12. faster
13. again
14. that (The sentence needs a word that refers to *things*.)
15. bad
16. Pomeray

Chapter 5
Guns, Guns, Too Many Guns?

Before You Read

Interview another person in your class. Ask them these questions.

1. What is your opinion of the use of guns?
2. Do you know anyone who has used guns?
3. Who in your country would need to own a gun?
4. Ask your own questions about guns.

Prereading Checklist

Before you start reading the passage "Guns, Guns, Too Many Guns?," skim it quickly looking for words you think might be important. Think about the illustration and the title. Try to get a general idea of what the passage is about.
    Now try to answer these questions. Discuss your answers with your classmates. Thinking about these questions will help prepare you to understand and enjoy what you read.

- Does this passage mainly tell a story or does it give information?
- Is the passage about the present, the past, or the future? Or is it a combination?
- Are there people in the passage? If so, what are their names, or what else can you find out about them?
- What are some words in the passage that seem to be important?
- After you discuss your answers, think about the illustration and the title again. Now, what do you think the passage is about? What do you already know about this topic?

Warm-Up

Strategy: Finding the Same Word in Another Context
When you see a word you don't know, and you cannot get the meaning from the context, look for the same word in another place in the reading. The next (or previous) time it is used there might be more clues about the meaning. This strategy can also help you guess the missing words in this book.

Example A

The lobby of the National Concert Hall is very beautiful. However, sometimes it is very noisy and full of cigarette smoke. This is because after a concert people like to go to the _____ and talk and smoke with friends.

lobby   stage   hall

Lobby is the correct word because the context tells you that it is part of a concert hall and a place to talk and smoke. Sometimes the same word is used in a different form, but the context will help you.

Example B

The novelist was very rich because many people bought the adventure _____ he wrote.

newspapers   pictures   novels

Novels is the correct choice because *novel* is part of *novelist,* and from the context you can see that novels have something to do with writing things that people enjoy reading.

Guns, Guns, Too Many Guns?

This reading is about guns and who should own and use them. First try to read and understand as much of the story as you can. Then look at the Word Choices section and try to guess the missing words. Finally, you can look at the vocabulary list for help with words you don't know.

Many people in the United States think that one of the biggest issues facing the country is the _____ (1) of gun control. Before the twentieth century, people owned guns because they needed them for their work or for their safety. People who worked in _____ (2) places carried guns for hunting and for protection against wild animals. Without guns, _____ (3) people could be killed or seriously hurt. Guns were not a hobby; nobody used them just for _____ (4). They were a _____ (5) part of daily life.

Now there are few people who need a gun for everyday life. Even the police in some _____ (6), such as England and Japan, only carry guns in emergencies. In almost every country there are now laws about who can own a gun. In some places the government made a _____ (7) that you can buy a rifle but not a pistol. In other places you can buy both. In some places it is difficult or impossible to buy a gun, but in others it is quite _____ (8).

Some people say that many criminals have guns, and we need to protect ourselves from these criminals. They also argue that guns should be sold to people who want to use them for hunting and target practice. These people believe that when people are not _____ (9) to own guns, they do not have true freedom. These people _____ (10) too much government control. Some people say that when people are free to own guns, they can feel safe from an unjust government.

32 / Guns, Guns, Too Many Guns?

Some people who want strict gun control argue that if guns are illegal, and only the police and the military have guns, the world will be safer. They say that many people are killed with guns _____ (11) accidents or during fights. It is a fact that hundreds of people are killed every week with guns, even in "peaceful" countries. Although many _____ (12) can be used to kill, relatively few people are killed with other weapons, such as knives. In the United States, where it is not difficult to buy a gun in most states, _____ (13) people, such as Martin Luther King and President John Kennedy, have been killed with guns.

These days everybody is talking about gun control. Both sides believe very strongly in their positions. Which _____ (14) do *you* support?

Word Choices

1. issue, answer, history
2. safe, enjoyable, dangerous
3. dangerous, unprotected, careful
4. fun, work, protection
5. pleasant, necessary, relaxed
6. states, counties, countries
7. hobby, chance, law
8. easy, difficult, illegal
9. limited, free, told
10. believe in, worry about, plan for
11. because of, in spite of, after
12. weapons, guns, people
13. poor, violent, famous
14. control, side, issue

Vocabulary

argue—give opinions strongly
criminals—people who do not obey the laws
emergencies—times of great danger
gun control—control of who is allowed to own a gun
military—people in the army, navy, or air force
pistol—a small gun
protection—keeping from danger, guarding
relatively—in comparison
rifle—a long gun
safety—being safe
side—opinion
strict gun control—allowing very few people to own guns
target practice—shooting a gun for practice
unjust—not fair, not honest

Comprehension Questions

1. What is one of the biggest issues in the United States today?
2. Can you buy a pistol and a rifle in every country?
3. Give two reasons why a person might want to own a gun.

34 / Guns, Guns, Too Many Guns?

4. If guns were illegal, who could still have a gun?
5. Which famous people in the U.S.A. have been killed with guns?

Questions for Discussion

1. What are the gun control laws in your country?
2. Are there many criminals with guns in your country?
3. What other arguments are there for and against owning guns?
4. Are people safer when they have guns?
5. Which side do you support in the gun control argument? Why?

Word Choices: Correct Answers

1. issue (The second time *issue* is used gives an example of what *issue* means.)
2. dangerous
3. unprotected (If guns are necessary for protection, people without guns will be *unprotected*.)
4. fun (*Fun* matches the same idea as *hobby*.)
5. necessary
6. countries (England and Japan are countries.)
7. law
8. easy (The word *but* is the clue.)
9. free (*Free* matches *freedom* in the next sentence.)
10. worry about
11. because of (People are killed and the *cause* is that someone had a gun.)
12. weapons (The next phrase mentions *weapons*.)
13. famous
14. side

Chapter 6
Two Kinds of Medicine

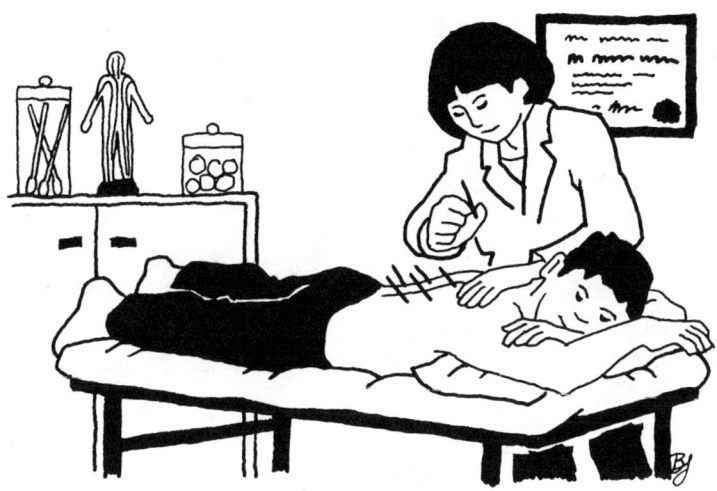

Before You Read

Every country has "folk" traditions. These are things people have done for hundreds of years. They might not be scientific, but many people believe in them. For example, some people eat one kind of food when they get sick, instead of going to the doctor or buying medicine.

Start a "Folk Tradition Dictionary" in your class. Each student can write a folk tradition from her/his country or culture. Later you might want to collect more of these and make a small book to share with other classes or visitors. You could also add drawings or pictures.

Prereading Checklist

Before you start reading the passage "Two Kinds of Medicine," skim it quickly looking for words you think might be important. Think about the illustration and the title. Try to get a general idea of what the passage is about.

Now try to answer these questions. Discuss your answers with your classmates. Thinking about these questions will help prepare you to understand and enjoy what you read.

36 / Two Kinds of Medicine

- Does this passage mainly tell a story or does it give information?
- Is the passage about the present, the past, or the future? Or is it a combination?
- Are there people in the passage? If so, what are their names, or what else can you find out about them?
- What are some words in the passage that seem to be important?
- After you discuss your answers, think about the illustration and the title again. Now, what do you think the passage is about? What do you already know about this topic?

Warm-Up

Strategy: Using Possessive Pronouns
In English, there are six possessive pronouns. They are: *my, your, its, her, his, our,* and *their.* To know which pronoun goes in a sentence, we have to look at the rest of the reading passage to see to which word the pronoun is connected. Let's look at two examples.

Example A

Yesterday Fumiko went to visit _____ grandfather.

                her   its   their

Her is the correct choice because Fumiko is one person.

Example B

Yesterday Saba went to visit her grandfather, but he wasn't in _____ house.

                her   his   your

His is the correct choice because it is the grandfather's house.

Two Kinds of Medicine

Dennis, who is from England, and Zhang, who is from China, are talking in York, a city in northern England. First try to read and understand as much of the story as you can. Then look at the Word Choices section and try to guess the missing words. Finally, you can look at the vocabulary list for help with words you don't know.

Dennis: Hi, Zhang.

Zhang: Hi, Dennis. You don't look very good today. Are you sick?

Dennis: _____ (1), I feel terrible.

Zhang: I'm _____ (2) to hear that. What's wrong with you?

Dennis: Every time I walk _____ (3) back hurts. Today I'm going to see a doctor.

Zhang: _____ (4) China, people with back pain have acupuncture.

Dennis: Acupuncture? _____ (5) that?

Zhang: Acupuncture is when a doctor puts long needles into _____ (6) body to help you feel better.

Dennis: Needles. Oh, you mean needles like doctors in England use to put medicine into a person's body?

Zhang: _____ (7). These needles are different. They do not have medicine in _____ (8). Also, sometimes doctors put many needles into a person at the same time to take away pain. For example, to take away back pain an acupuncture doctor puts needles in your foot and in your neck.

Dennis: Wow!

Two Kinds of Medicine

Zhang: You see, in China today we have two kinds of medicine. One kind _____ (9) thousands of years old. This is called traditional medicine. Traditional doctors use plants and trees to make _____ (10) medicine. And, they use acupuncture. The _____ (11) kind of medicine we have in China is modern medicine. This is new. The doctors here in England also use modern medicine. Today in China _____ (12) doctors use both modern and traditional medicine together.

Dennis: Please tell me some more about traditional medicine.

Zhang: Um . . . when I have a cold and my throat hurts, I use traditional medicine that looks like a small ball. I put the _____ (13) ball in a cup and fill _____ (14) cup with hot water. The water makes the ball grow bigger. The ball grows bigger and bigger, and _____ (15) medicine comes out of the ball and into the water. I drink the water, and it helps make the cold go away.

Dennis: The little ball sounds like fun.

Zhang: It is fun to watch the ball get bigger in the water, but the medicine doesn't taste good.

Dennis: Yeah, I'm afraid that traditional and modern medicine both taste _____ (16).

Zhang: Yes, but acupuncture doesn't hurt much. Maybe you can go to an acupuncture doctor for your back.

Dennis: That's a good idea. Today in England the doctors are studying traditional medicine from many countries. Maybe I can find an acupuncture doctor _____ (17).

Word Choices

1. No, Therefore, Yes
2. better, sorry, glad
3. my, the, your
4. At, On, In
5. Who's, Where's, What's
6. his, its, your
7. No, Therefore, Yes
8. it, you, them
9. was, is, will be
10. their, there, they're
11. also, other, another
12. our, their, your
13. big, old, little
14. the, big, a
15. basketball, its, your
16. delicious, good, bad
17. there, good, here

Vocabulary

medicine—something you eat or drink when you are sick to make you better
needles—thin pieces of metal with a point at one end
traditional—doing things in ways that began many, many years ago

Comprehension Questions

1. Why does Dennis feel terrible?
2. Does Zhang have a cold now?
3. Does Dennis like to take medicine?
4. Many years ago, which kind of medicine was most popular in China, traditional or modern?
5. Which kind of medicine is most popular today in England?
6. Which kind of medicine is in the little ball—traditional or modern?

Questions for Discussion

1. Do you want to try acupuncture?
2. Do you know other kinds of traditional medicine?
3. Have you used traditional medicine?
4. What do you do when you have a cold?
5. Are traditional and modern medicine both useful? Explain your answer.

Word Choices: Correct Answers

1. Yes
2. sorry
3. my (It is Dennis's back that hurts.)
4. In
5. What's
6. your (The doctor puts the needle into *you*.)
7. No
8. them
9. is
10. their (The other choices are pronounced the same, but have different meanings, and they are not possessive pronouns.)
11. other
12. our (Zhang is from China.)
13. little
14. the
15. its (The ball's medicine comes out.)
16. bad
17. here

Chapter 7
Learning about Other Countries without Leaving Home

Before You Read

In a group, you name countries you have never visited but which you want to visit. Say why you want to visit the countries, what you already know about them, and how you learned about the countries (for example: in school, from friends, from television or movies).

Prereading Checklist

Before you start reading the passage "Learning about Other Countries without Leaving Home," skim it quickly looking for words you think might be important. Think about the illustration and the title. Try to get a general idea of what the passage is about.

Now try to answer these questions. Discuss your answers with your classmates. Thinking about these questions will help prepare you to understand and enjoy what you read.

44 / Learning about Other Countries

- Does this passage mainly tell a story or does it give information?
- Is the passage about the present, the past, or the future? Or is it a combination?
- Are there people in the passage? If so, what are their names, or what else can you find out about them?
- What are some words in the passage that seem to be important?
- After you discuss your answers, think about the illustration and the title again. Now, what do you think the passage is about? What do you already know about this topic?

Warm-Up

Strategy: Connecting Ideas Using *And* and *But*

And and *but* are words we use to join together other words. We usually use *and* to join together thoughts that agree. We use *but* to join together words or sentences that show two different ideas.

Example A

Greek is a difficult language, _____ Susan learned it in two months.

and   but

But is probably the best choice, because when you read "difficult language" you would not think someone could learn it in two months, so the ideas are different.

Example B

Greek is a difficult language, _____ Susan had to study it for ten years before she learned it.

and   but

And is probably the best choice now, because what you think when you read "difficult language" and "had to study it for ten years" agree.

To understand if two ideas agree, we need to understand the main ideas of the author. When you read the story, think about the main ideas of the paragraphs and the passage. This will help you correctly choose *and* or *but*.

Learning about Other Countries without Leaving Home

This story is about a man who learned about life in a foreign country without leaving home. First try to read and understand as much of the story as you can. Then look at the Word Choices section and try to guess the missing words. Finally, you can look at the vocabulary list for help with words you don't know.

Jerry Mercer always wanted to visit a foreign country, _____ (1) he did not have much money. Jerry lived with his parents on a small vegetable farm in a small town in the United States. Many of Jerry's friends went away to college after high school, _____ (2) Jerry stayed home to help his father work on the farm. In the evenings, Jerry _____ (3) books about travel and adventure in distant places or went to adventure movies, and dreamed about seeing the world.

Life on the farm was difficult, _____ (4) Jerry's father was often sick. So Jerry had to work hard every day. One day he read an article in a _____ (5) about some immigrants from Southeast Asia who were living in his town. It was not easy for them to feel comfortable in the United States. The immigrants were poor, did not speak English well, _____ (6) were unfamiliar with life in the United States.

Jerry decided to meet some of these _____ (7). Maybe he could help them learn English and learn about life in the United States, _____ (8) maybe they could teach him about life in another part of the world. Soon Jerry met the Truan family from Laos.

At first, Jerry and the Truans had a lot of trouble understanding each other because of language problems and cultural differences, _____ (9) they soon became friends, _____ (10) they began to understand each other better. When the Truans and Jerry found differences between Laotian and American cultures, they were all able to learn more about _____ (11) way of life.

For example, when Jerry's father died, the Truans learned about what death means for Americans, _____ (12) when Grandmother Truan died, Jerry learned about what death means for Laotians. They learned about each other's culture; but they kept their own.

Jerry never did _____ (13) foreign countries. After his father died, he was _____ (14) too busy on the farm. He could not travel, _____ (15) he learned more than most travelers do about life in distant places from his friendship with the Truans.

Word Choices

1. and, but
2. and, but
3. read, reads, will read
4. and, but
5. book, movie, newspaper
6. and, but
7. countries, farms, immigrants
8. and, but
9. and, but
10. and, but
11. a better, another, the same
12. and, but
13. learn about, like, visit
14. always, never
15. and, but

Vocabulary

article—something written in a magazine or newspaper
distant—far away
immigrants—people who move to a new country
unfamiliar with—not knowing about

Comprehension Questions

1. What job did Jerry have?
2. Did Jerry go to college? Why or why not?
3. Did Jerry meet the Truans in the United States or in Laos?
4. Why did the immigrants feel uncomfortable in the United States?
5. Why was it difficult for Jerry and the Truans to understand each other at first?

Questions for Discussion

1. Are there immigrants in your country? If there are, what problems do they have?
2. What are important things that immigrants in your country need to know about your country's culture?

48 / Learning about Other Countries

3. What are some ways to solve communication problems?
4. Is it possible to learn about other cultures and keep your own, or do you lose your culture when you learn about other cultures?
5. Jerry never visited another country, but he learned more than most travelers about life in other countries. How is that possible?
6. Can you also learn about life in other countries in the same way that Jerry did? What other ways are there to learn about culture without traveling?

Word Choices: Correct Answers

1. but (Travel and "not much money" don't agree.)
2. but (They left; he didn't.)
3. read
4. and (Bad health and a difficult life often go together.)
5. newspaper
6. and (These ideas are similar.)
7. immigrants
8. and (They would learn *and* he would learn.)
9. but (Trouble and friendship don't agree.)
10. and (Friendship and understanding agree.)
11. another
12. and (Both events refer to death.)
13. visit
14. always
15. but (He was busy *but* he learned.)

Chapter 8
Is There Enough Food in the World for Everyone?

Before You Read

Interview one of your classmates. Ask the following questions about food. Then let your classmate interview you. Share your answers with the class.

- What's your favorite food?
- How often do you eat your favorite food?
- What food do you like least?
- Is there a food for which your country or hometown is famous?

Prereading Checklist

Before you start reading the passage "Is There Enough Food in the World for Everyone?" skim it quickly looking for words you think might be important. Think about the illustration and the title. Try to get a general idea of what the passage is about.

50 / Is There Enough Food in the World?

Now try to answer these questions. Discuss your answers with your classmates. Thinking about these questions will help prepare you to understand and enjoy what you read.

- Does this passage mainly tell a story or does it give information?
- Is the passage about the present, the past, or the future? Or is it a combination?
- Are there people in the passage? If so, what are their names, or what else can you find out about them?
- What are some words in the passage that seem to be important?
- After you discuss your answers, think about the illustration and the title again. Now, what do you think the passage is about? What do you already know about this topic?

Warm-Up

Strategy: Getting Help from Other Paragraphs
Sometimes the information you need to fill a blank is in the same sentence or in another sentence in the same paragraph. However, other times you will need to use information from another paragraph to fill a blank. That paragraph may be before or after the one you are reading.

Example

Read both paragraphs before trying to fill the blanks.

Saturday was very hot, and five-year-old Cheng was thirsty. So, she asked her mother for some money to buy some drinks at the store for herself and her brothers and sisters. Cheng was walking to the store when something _____ happened.

good   sad

Cheng lost the money. The _____ walked slowly back home looking for the money, did not find it, and started to cry.

man   boy   girl   woman

Sad is the correct choice in the first blank because the next paragraph tells us that Cheng lost her money and was crying. *Girl* is the correct choice in the second blank because the first paragraph tells us that Cheng was five years old, and the words *she* and *her* tell us that Cheng was female, not male.

Is There Enough Food in the World for Everyone?

In many places in the world, even in rich countries, there are people who don't have enough to eat. This reading is about some of the reasons for hunger in the world. First, try to read and understand as much of the passage as you can. Then look at the Word Choices section and try to guess the missing words. Finally, you can look at the vocabulary list for help with words you don't know.

It is sad to know that millions of people die every year because they do not have enough food. This lack of food makes people weak. When people are weak they die easily from disease and other causes. _____ (1) don't people have enough food?

The main reason that we hear to explain hunger is, "There is not enough food in the world for everyone." Is this true? Is there not enough food? The facts show that it is _____ (2).

The facts show that the world produces more than enough food for everyone to have all the food they need to be healthy. Although the world's population has grown rapidly, food production has grown _____ (3) than the population. Where does all this food go?

Every day, large amounts of food _____ (4) thrown away in rich countries. Why don't people in rich countries send food to people in poor countries? The answer to this _____ (5) is not easy. Here are _____ (6) reasons.

First, it is not easy to just put extra food in a box and mail it to a hungry person in another country. Food is heavy and sending it is expensive. Second, some people in _____ (7) countries think that hungry people will become lazy and not work if other people send them food. A third reason people _____ (8) help the hungry is that they want to keep food and money for themselves.

Although it is hard to believe, in some countries food is exported to other countries at the same time that people go hungry. For example, in India there are many hungry people. Yet India _____ (9) many food products, such as wheat and meat.

Why is food exported from countries where people are hungry? _____ (10), the answer is not easy. Countries export food because they need money to pay for imports. If a country has no exports, it cannot have many _____ (11).

_____ (12), hungry people have little money to buy food. Companies in the international food business cannot make any money if they give food to hungry people who have no money. Without money, they cannot pay their workers or have a successful business. _____ (13) they sell food to other countries.

The problem of hunger is one of the most important problems in the world today. Each year, hunger causes _____ (14) of deaths. There is enough food in the world to feed everyone, but it is not easy to get food to everyone who needs it.

54 / Is There Enough Food in the World?

Word Choices

1. When, Where, Why
2. false, true
3. faster, slower
4. are, is
5. example, reason, question
6. three, four, five
7. big, rich, small
8. can, do, do not
9. buys, exports, produces
10. Again, However, Therefore
11. food products, hungry people, imports
12. Additionally, First, Therefore
13. Additionally, However, Therefore
14. billions, millions, thousands

Vocabulary

export—send to other countries
extra—additional, not necessary
fact—something that is true
healthy—well, not sick
imports—products bought from other countries
lazy—like a person who does not like to work
population—number of people
produces—makes or grows

Comprehension Questions

1. How does hunger kill people?
2. Is there enough food in the world to feed everyone?
3. Is it true or false that food production has grown faster than the population?
4. Why do some countries export food instead of using the food to help hungry people in their own country?
5. Why is hunger a difficult problem for international food companies?

Questions for Discussion

1. What reasons have you heard to explain hunger in the world?
2. If people with food and money do not help hungry people, does this mean that they are bad people? If you answer yes, what should they do to help hungry people?
3. If hungry people receive food from other people, will the hungry people become lazy?
4. Are there hungry people where you live? How can other people help hungry people?
5. Have you ever gone for several days without enough food? Tell your classmates about your experience.
6. Is it possible to end hunger in the world? If so, how?

Word Choices: Correct Answers

1. Why (The next paragraph is about the main *reason* people give to explain hunger.)
2. false (The next paragraph says that the world produces more than enough food to feed everyone.)
3. faster
4. are (The subject of the sentence is *amounts*.)
5. question
6. three (The next paragraph gives three reasons.)
7. rich (This paragraph answers the question from the previous paragraph about people in rich countries.)
8. do not
9. exports
10. Again (In paragraph 4 the author said, "The answer to this question is not easy.")
11. imports
12. Additionally (The previous paragraph gives one reason why countries with hungry people export food. This paragraph gives an *additional* reason.)
13. Therefore
14. millions (The first paragraph tells us this.)

Chapter 9
Two Friends with Different Futures

Before You Read

In the United States, there are many different groups of people called Native Americans. You have probably heard of American Indians and Eskimos. What do you know about Native Americans? With your classmates, make a list of what you know. How did you learn about Native Americans? Do you think your information is complete and correct? How could you get more information about Native Americans?

Prereading Checklist

Before you start reading the passage "Two Friends with Different Futures," skim it quickly looking for words you think might be important. Think about the illustration and the title. Try to get a general idea of what the passage is about.

Now try to answer these questions. Discuss your answers with your classmates. Thinking about these questions will help prepare you to understand and enjoy what you read.

58 / Two Friends with Different Futures

- Does this passage mainly tell a story or does it give information?
- Is the passage about the present, the past, or the future? Or is it a combination?
- Are there people in the passage? If so, what are their names, or what else can you find out about them?
- What are some words in the passage that seem to be important?
- After you discuss your answers, think about the illustration and the title again. Now, what do you think the passage is about? What do you already know about this topic?

Warm-Up

Strategy: Using Infinitives
Often in English we use a verb with the preposition *to*. This is often done when we combine two verbs. This pattern—*to* + *verb*—is called an *infinitive*. Look at this sentence.

Larry learned how to sail a boat.

Learned and *sail* are the verbs, and *to sail* is the infinitive.
    When we use infinitives, we always use the dictionary form of the verb, that is, the present, singular form. Look at the following sentences showing incorrect and correct ways to use the infinitive.

[Incorrect] He started to talked.
[Correct] He started to talk.

[Incorrect] Chung Yuk is studying to entering college.
[Correct] Chung Yuk is studying to enter college.

    Try these examples.

Example A

Barry was excited to _____ at his new school.

arrive   *arrival*   *arriving*

Arrive is the correct choice because it is the present, singular form of the verb.

Example B

Forgetting how to _____ the lock was Tsu Chai's biggest mistake.

opening   *open*   *opened*

Open is the present, singular form of the verb.

Two Friends with Different Futures

This reading is about two women who are similar in some ways but have very different plans. First try to read and understand as much of the story as you can. Then look at the Word Choices section and try to guess the missing words. Finally, you can look at the vocabulary list for help with words you don't know.

Two young women met at college. Both of them were studying education at the University of Alaska, in Juneau, Alaska. Alaska is the biggest state in the United States. They _____ (1) were members of the same group of Native Americans, the Yup'ik Eskimos. There are many Yup'iks in Alaska, and they live in many parts of that _____ (2).

_____ (3) of the young women, Elena, was born in Fairbanks, the largest city in Alaska. She _____ (4) there all her life. She could speak only a little of the Yup'ik language, although her parents spoke it. The other woman, Shelly, was from a small town in the country. Her family made money by fishing and farming. Shelly spoke both the Yup'ik language and English very well. She had learned _____ (5) English in school. In her village everyone spoke Yup'ik in day-to-day life.

After the first few weeks of school, the two women became good friends, and often _____ (6) about their dreams and plans. Elena wanted to teach in a large private school for a few years, and then _____ (7) her own business. She loved life in the city, because in the city she could go to the movies, travel easily, buy modern things, and have a _____ (8) life. Shelly, on the other hand, wanted to go back to her town and work in the small school there after graduation. She knew that very few teachers in Alaska know how to speak the Yup'ik language, so Shelly _____ (9) she could use both Yup'ik and English to help the children learn.

Shelly wanted to help the children learn about their native culture. She thought this would help the children to _____ (10) their lives. She also wanted to keep the native culture and traditions of her people strong. Life in the small town in the country was _____ (11), but she did not want to live in the city.

Sometimes the young women talked about how difficult it is to _____ (12) from two cultures, that of the United States and that of the _____ (13). Both of the women knew that the world was changing quickly for Native Americans. They were proud of their country and their Yup'ik culture, but they each had _____ (14) a choice about their future. Elena worried that if she lived like people in the rest of the United States she would not be a Native American. Shelly worried that after she _____ (15) to her town she would not experience very much of the modern world.

Word Choices

1. both, neither, none
2. country, island, state
3. Two, Both, One
4. lived, to live, living
5. talking, to study, to speak
6. to talk, talked, talking
7. start, starting, started
8. uncomfortable, comfortable, unhappy
9. taught, thought, forgot
10. forget, improve, escape
11. easy, modern, difficult
12. be, is, are
13. city, Eskimo, American
14. make, making, to make
15. to return, returning, returned

Vocabulary

country—outside of the city, an area with few buildings and few people
day-to-day—normal, usual, everyday
Native Americans—people who lived in America before the Europeans came. Eskimos and American Indians are Native Americans.
native culture—the old ways and customs of a group of people such as American Indians
on the other hand—in contrast, in a different way

Comprehension Questions

1. Who are the Yup'ik Eskimos? Where do they live?
2. Where were the two women born?
3. Who could speak Yup'ik better, Elena or Shelly?
4. What were the two women's plans for the future?
5. How could Shelly help the Yup'ik children in her village?

Two Friends with Different Futures / 63

Questions for Discussion

1. Shelly is very proud of her Yup'ik culture. What things in your culture are *you* most proud of?
2. What things in other cultures do you admire?
3. At your school, what do you learn that is modern, and what do you learn that is traditional?
4. Some people are more interested in business careers and making money, and some are more interested in helping others. Is it possible to do both—help others *and* make money? Explain your answer.
5. What are your career plans? What is important to *you* in planning your career?

Word Choices: Correct Answers

1. both
2. state (Alaska is a state in the country of the United States.)
3. One (The sentence is only about Elena.)
4. lived
5. to speak
6. talked
7. start
8. comfortable (Elena *loved* life in the city because it was comfortable.)
9. thought
10. improve
11. difficult
12. be
13. Eskimo (*Yup'ik* would also be a good answer.)
14. to make
15. returned

Chapter 10
Clean Water and the Women of Burkina Faso

Before You Read

Work in groups of three or four people. Take out a piece of paper—so in a group of three there will be three pieces of paper. Each group is going to make lists of ways to use water. On your paper, write one way to use water. Be specific. Then, give your paper to another person in your group. Next, write a reason on your new paper and give it to another person in your group. At the end, each group will have three lists of ways to use water. Finally, the whole class can look for similarities and differences between the groups' lists.

Prereading Checklist

Before you start reading the passage "Clean Water and the Women of Burkina Faso," skim it quickly looking for words you think might be important. Think about the illustration and the title. Try to get a general idea of what the passage is about.

Now try to answer these questions. Discuss your answers with your classmates. Thinking about these questions will help prepare you to understand and enjoy what you read.

- Does this passage mainly tell a story or does it give information?
- Is the passage about the present, the past, or the future? Or is it a combination?
- Are there people in the passage? If so, what are their names, or what else can you find out about them?
- What are some words in the passage that seem to be important?
- After you discuss your answers, think about the illustration and the title again. Now, what do you think the passage is about? What do you already know about this topic?

Warm-Up

Strategy: Connecting Ideas Using *Additionally*, *Although*, and *Because*

When we connect two parts of a sentence or we connect two sentences, we use *connectors*. *Additionally*, *although*, and *because* are three of these connectors. Each one of these connectors gives us different information about how ideas connect together.

Additionally is similar to *also*. It is used to add an idea that is similar to one already stated in the reading passage. *Although* usually shows contrast between two parts of a sentence. *Because* answers the question "why?" It gives us reasons.

Let's look at three examples.

Example A

People from Pakistan went to Kuwait to work. _____ , Pakistanis worked in the oil industry of Saudi Arabia.

Additionally   *Although*   *Because*

Additionally is the correct choice because the first sentence tells us that people from Pakistan worked in Kuwait, and the second sentence *adds* that Pakistanis also went to Saudi Arabia to work.

Example B

_____ Saudi Arabia makes a lot of money from selling oil, the country has many modern buildings.

Additionally   Although   Because

Because is the correct choice because selling oil is one of the *reasons* Saudi Arabia has the money to build modern buildings.

Example C

_____ thousands of Pakistanis go to work in Saudi Arabia, many of them will return to Pakistan.

Additionally   Although   Because

Although is the correct choice because there is a contrast between the two parts of the sentence. In the first part the Pakistanis leave their own country to work in a foreign country: Saudi Arabia. The second part of the sentence tells us that they will go back to Pakistan.

Clean Water and the Women of Burkina Faso

For some of us, getting water is easy. We push a button or turn a faucet, and the water comes to us. But for others of us, getting water is not easy. This is a story about what a group of people did to get water more easily.

First, try to read and understand as much of the passage as you can. Then look at the Word Choices section and try to guess the missing words. Finally, you can look at the vocabulary list for help with words you don't know.

Water is important to us in many ways. We use water for drinking, washing, and farming, and in many other ways. But, sometimes there is not enough clean water for everyone. _____ (1) water covers 70 percent of the earth, only 3 percent of this water is fresh water; the rest is salt water, mostly from the ocean. _____ (2), pollution has made a lot of water too dirty for people to use.

_____ (3) of the importance of water, the United Nations (UN) made the ten years 1981—90 an international clean water decade. The UN wanted to help everyone _____ (4) clean water. _____ (5), the UN wanted everyone to have an easy way to get water. Unfortunately, many people have to carry water a long distance _____ (6) they do not have water in their homes.

In Burkina Faso, a country in western Africa, it is usually the women who have to _____ (7) the water to their homes. In the village of Saye in Burkina Faso the water problem was especially bad when there was not much rain. _____ (8) the government and the men of the village did not solve the problem, the women of Saye had to organize a meeting to talk about how to get more water. They decided to build a dam to catch the water that came during the rainy season.

Building a dam is a big job, so _____ (9) people from other villages came to Saye to help. _____ (10) they did not have modern equipment, they finally finished building the dam. A few hours after the dam was finished, the first rains of the year came to Saye. The women were so happy! On that day, there _____ (11) a big celebration with eating, _____ (12), and singing.

_____ (13) the women of Saye still work hard to take care of their families, life is now a little easier for them _____ (14) of the new dam. The women saw that they could change their _____ (15) lives; they did not have to wait for men or the government to help them.

Word Choices

1. Additionally, Although, Because
2. Additionally, Although, Because
3. Additionally, Although, Because
4. had, has, have
5. Additionally, Although, Because
6. additionally, although, because
7. carry, drink, wash
8. Additionally, Although, Because
9. few, hundreds of, no
10. Additionally, Although, Because
11. is, was, will be
12. dancing, studying, testing
13. Additionally, Although, Because
14. additionally, although, because
15. government's, men's, own

Vocabulary

dam—barrier built to hold back water
equipment—tools and machines
especially—very
faucet—a pipe from which we can get water
pollution—something that makes water, air, etc., dirty
sanitation—cleanliness
solve—find the answer to

Comprehension Questions

1. What percent of the earth is covered by *land*?
2. What are two reasons why the UN made 1981–90 an international clean water decade?
3. Who usually brings the water to the homes in Burkina Faso?
4. What did the people build in Saye?
5. What two things happened on the day when the dam was finished?

Clean Water / 71

Questions for Discussion

1. How do you get your water? How did your grandparents get their water when they were young?
2. What are some different ways that water gets dirty?
3. Is the water that you drink clean? Could it be cleaner? If so, how?
4. In Saye, the women carried the water. Which jobs in your country are usually women's jobs? Which jobs are men's jobs? Why?
5. The women in Saye worked together to help solve a difficult problem. Did you ever work with a big or small group to solve a difficult problem?

Word Choices: Correct Answers

1. Although (The sentence shows the *contrast* between the large amount of water and the small amount of fresh water.)
2. Additionally (Pollution is an *additional* reason why there is not enough water for everyone.)
3. Because (The importance of water is *why* the UN made 1981–90 a special clean water decade.)
4. have
5. Additionally (The UN wanted *two things:* clean water *and* water that is convenient, easy to get.)
6. because (The *reason* people have to carry water is that there is no water in their homes.)
7. carry
8. Because (The *reason* the women had to organize a meeting was that no one else was solving the problem.)
9. hundreds of
10. Although (There is a *contrast* between not having modern equipment to build the dam and being able to finish such a big job.)
11. was
12. dancing
13. Although (There is a *contrast* between easy and hard.)
14. because (The new dam is the *reason* life is a little easier.)
15. own

Chapter 11
Can the Rain Forest Be Saved?

Before You Read

Recently, more and more people want to help save the environment. List things that you do now or that you can do to help save the environment. Do this alone or in a group. Then, discuss your ideas with the rest of the class.

Prereading Checklist

Before you start reading the passage "Can the Rain Forest Be Saved," skim it quickly looking for words you think might be important. Think about the illustration and the title. Try to get a general idea of what the passage is about.

Now try to answer these questions. Discuss your answers with your classmates. Thinking about these questions will help prepare you to understand and enjoy what you read.

- Does this passage mainly tell a story or does it give information?
- Is the passage about the present, the past, or the future? Or is it a combination?

74 / Can the Rain Forest Be Saved?

- Are there people in the passage? If so, what are their names, or what else can you find out about them?
- What are some words in the passage that seem to be important?
- After you discuss your answers, think about the illustration and the title again. Now, what do you think the passage is about? What do you already know about this topic?

Warm-Up

Strategy: Linking Cause and Effect
When you read carefully, you can often see that the information in two sentences is connected. One sentence tells why the information in the other sentence is true. One sentence gives the *cause,* and the other sentence gives the *effect*.

Example A

Marcel lost all of his money at the horse race. His father was very

_____ .

happy   tired   angry

Angry is the correct answer. His father's anger was *caused* by Marcel's gambling.

Example B

Lionel reads a lot of newspapers. This _____ his knowledge of world events.

improves   hurts

Improves is the answer because reading a lot has the *effect* of improving knowledge of world events.

Can the Rain Forest Be Saved?

This reading is about the rain forests in the Amazon area of Brazil and one man who tried to protect the trees there. First try to read and understand as much of the story as you can. Then look at the Word Choices section and try to guess the missing words. Finally, you can look at the vocabulary list for help with words you don't know.

The Amazon River in South America is nearly 6,500 kilometers (almost 4,000 miles) long. It is the second _____ (1) river in the world. (The Nile, in Africa, is longest.) The Amazon goes through eight countries, but most of it is in the country of Brazil. Around the river is the world's biggest forest. It is called a "rain forest" because of the heavy _____ (2) that makes the forest tall and _____ (3). It covers seven million square kilometers (2.7 million square miles). More than a million kinds of plants and animals live there.

Although Indians lived in the rain forest for a long time, about four hundred years _____ (4) other people started to go into the forest and _____ (5) the trees. They wanted to make farms or ranches or to get wood. Recently this problem has become much more serious. In just _____ (6), 1988, over thirty-one thousand square kilometers (over twelve thousand square miles) of rain forest were cut or burned.

An expert on the Amazon area says that unless things change, the forest will disappear. If the forest does disappear, it will be very _____ (7) for the whole world, not only Brazil. Plants and animals would _____ (8), and the Indians could not live there. However, the worst problem might be that fewer rain clouds over the Amazon could make the whole earth warmer. This is part of what is called the "greenhouse effect." It could melt the ice at the north and south poles and _____ (9) the ocean level around the world.

One _____ (10) person who tried to stop people from cutting the trees was Chico Mendes. He was a leader of rubber tappers in the Brazilian state of Acre. Rubber tappers collect rubber from trees in the rain forest. They can get rubber out of rubber trees without cutting or killing the trees. Chico and other rubber tappers tried to stop ranchers and farmers from cutting trees to clear the land, and they tried to stop the government from building roads that bring _____ (11) people into the forest. If the trees are cut, the rubber tappers lose their jobs.

But the ranchers and farmers wanted to cut down the trees so they could have more land to raise cattle and grow food. Sometimes, the ranchers and farmers used violence against the people who tried to stop them. Chico knew he was in great danger, and one day he was shot and killed in his home. A rancher was sent to prison for _____ (12) him.

Can the rain forest be saved? Yes it can, but it will not be easy. The countries of the Amazon area must _____ (13) encouraging people to clear the forest land. They must also build fewer dams, which also _____ (14) the forest by covering it with water. But it is also important that all of the countries of the world help. They must set a good example for the future of the Amazon. One way they can help is by _____ (15) the pollution in their own countries and saving their own forests and rivers.

Word Choices

1. longest, shortest
2. water, rain, snow
3. thick, thin, weak
4. now, then, ago
5. grow, cut, save
6. two years, six months, one year
7. bad, good
8. die, live, move
9. lower, reduce, raise
10. weak, government, brave
11. Indian, fewer, more
12. killing, watching, protecting
13. start, continue, stop
14. save, strengthen, kill
15. increasing, reducing, doubling

Vocabulary

dam—a wall built on a lake or rivers to collect the water or to make electricity
disappear—be gone
encourage—make someone want to do something
expert—a person who knows a lot about a particular topic
forest—a large area with many trees
melt—turn ice into water
north and south poles—the areas at the top and bottom of the earth which are mostly covered with ice
pollution—dirty air, land, and water
prison—a place for people who break laws
ranch—a large farm for raising animals
reduce—make less
set a good example—show a good way to do things
violence—force used against people to hurt them, especially with a gun or other weapon

78 / Can the Rain Forest Be Saved?

Comprehension Questions

1. How long is the longest river in South America?
2. Why is the Amazon forest called a "rain forest"?
3. Has the clearing of the rain forest always been a problem?
4. What is one of the causes of the "greenhouse effect"?
5. Why was Chico Mendes killed?

Questions for Discussion

1. Are there fewer forests or other wild areas in your country today than twenty years ago?
2. In addition to the reasons given in the reading passage, what are some other reasons to save the Amazon forests?
3. What reasons do you think the ranchers and farmers in the Amazon give for clearing the trees?
4. Has pollution changed your country? How? Is the air in your country clean?
5. What would happen if the level of the oceans became higher?
6. Was Chico Mendes a hero? What else do you want to know about him?

Word Choices: Correct Answers

1. longest
2. rain
3. thick (The heavy rain *causes* the trees to get thick.)
4. ago
5. cut (The need for wood or land *caused* them to cut the trees.)
6. one year (1988 is one year.)
7. bad
8. die
9. raise (More water in the ocean will *cause* the level to rise.)
10. brave (A weak person would not fight, and Mendes fought *against* the government's plans.)
11. more (Roads cause more people to come. The Indians are already there.)
12. killing
13. stop
14. kill (The *effect* of dams is to cover the land and kill the trees.)
15. reducing (Reducing the pollution will have the *effect* of setting a good example.)

Chapter 12
Are Languages Alive?

Before You Read

Think about your own language. Are there any new words? Are there any words you use that your parents didn't use when they were young?

Make a list of some of these new words. Try to translate them into English and then share them with your classmates.

Prereading Checklist

Before you start reading the passage "Are Languages Alive?" skim it quickly looking for words you think might be important. Think about the illustration and the title. Try to get a general idea of what the passage is about.

Now try to answer these questions. Discuss your answers with your classmates. Thinking about these questions will help prepare you to understand and enjoy what you read.

- Does this passage mainly tell a story or does it give information?
- Is the passage about the present, the past, or the future? Or is it a combination?

80 / Are Languages Alive?

- Are there people in the passage? If so, what are their names, or what else can you find out about them?
- What are some words in the passage that seem to be important?
- After you discuss your answers, think about the illustration and the title again. Now, what do you think the passage is about? What do you already know about this topic?

Warm-Up

Strategy: Using Words of Quantity

When we want to refer to a quantity, we often use the words *many, much,* and *no. Many* and *much* mean the same thing, but they are used with different kinds of nouns.

Many is only used with "count" nouns (you often make these plural by adding "s").

I saw *many* ducks in the lake.

Much is used with "noncount" nouns.

There is too *much* salt in the soup.

Try these examples yourself.

Example A

This history lesson is too _____ work.

much   many   no

Much is the correct choice because *history* is a noncount noun.

Example B

I spent all of my money. I have _____ more.

much   many   no

No is the correct choice. *Money* is usually used as a noncount noun.

Example C

People go to _____ places for vacations, but I can't because I spent all my money!

much   many   no

Many is the correct choice because *places* is a count noun.

Are Languages Alive?

This passage is about language and how it changes. First, try to read and understand as much of the passage as you can. Then look at the Word Choices section and try to guess the missing words. Finally, you can look at the vocabulary list for help with the words you don't know.

Some people say that languages are alive _____ (1) they are always changing. A language that stops changing becomes a "dead language." Languages change in _____ (2) ways. We add new words _____ (3) year to our languages, and the meanings of some old words change. For example, when you _____ (4) the word *keyboard,* do you think of a piano or a computer? Today, _____ (5) people think of a computer keyboard. Many of the words that are used every day in _____ (6) languages were not used in that way a few years ago. Words and phrases that used to be called slang, like *spacey* or *dropout,* are now used by almost _____ (7).

All languages change, and every generation adds new words and also _____ (8) meanings to a language. The Japanese recently started to use the word *pasokon.* This is a short form of the English term *personal computer.* Some people complain that using these new words is a bad _____ (9). They think that all languages should be kept pure, and there should be no foreign _____ (10) or slang.

However, _____ (11) language is completely pure. For example, _____ (12) of English comes from foreign languages, such as Latin, German, and French. In fact, English began in Germany, not in _____ (13).

No language is pure, and we must accept that _____ (14)

change is inevitable. We _____ (15) keep our languages from changing, even if we try. We should enjoy learning new ways to speak and write, or we will be left behind!

Word Choices

1. although, despite, because
2. many, much, no
3. each, many, phrases
4. hear, understand, think
5. many, much, no
6. future, dead, modern
7. none, everyone, friends
8. new, incorrect, another
9. speech, sentence, idea
10. food, languages, words
11. many, much, no
12. many, much, no
13. France, foreign, England
14. many, much, no
15. cannot, should, never

Vocabulary

be left behind—do things in an old way, not modern
complain—say that something is wrong
dropout—a slang word for a student who stops going to school
generation—all people who are about the same age
inevitable—certain, sure to happen
pure—not mixed with anything
slang—new words and phrases that are popular among some groups of people but are not used in formal speech
spacey—a slang word meaning foolish

Comprehension Questions

1. What is a "dead language"?
2. Which English slang words are now used by almost everybody?
3. What does *pasokon* mean?
4. Which languages do many English words come from?
5. Is it possible to keep a language from changing?

Questions for Discussion

1. What are some examples of changes in your native language?
2. What words that come from other languages have been added to your language? Is the meaning of the words the same in the original language?
3. Do you use slang? What do people think about slang in your native language?
4. When foreign words are added to a language, should we try to pronounce them the way foreigners do?
5. In some countries, people try to stop foreign words from coming into their language. Do you think this is a good idea? Discuss why it would be hard to keep any language pure.

Word Choices: Correct Answers

1. because
2. many (*Ways* is plural.)
3. each
4. hear
5. many (*People* has a plural meaning.)
6. modern
7. everyone
8. new
9. idea
10. words
11. no (Look at the first sentence of the last paragraph.)
12. much (*English* is a "noncount" noun.)
13. England
14. much (*Change* is singular.)
15. cannot

Chapter 13
Where Have All the Young People Gone?

Before You Read

Many people live on small islands. What small island countries can you name?
 Often these islands are hundreds of kilometers from larger bodies of land. How do you think life is different in these countries from life in other countries? Have you ever been to a small island country?

Prereading Checklist

Before you start reading the passage "Where Have All the Young People Gone?" skim it quickly looking for words you think might be important. Think about the illustration and the title. Try to get a general idea of what the passage is about.
 Now try to answer these questions. Discuss your answers with your classmates. Thinking about these questions will help prepare you to understand and enjoy what you read.

88 / Where Have All the Young People Gone?

- Does this passage mainly tell a story or does it give information?
- Is the passage about the present, the past, or the future? Or is it a combination?
- Are there people in the passage? If so, what are their names, or what else can you find out about them?
- What are some words in the passage that seem to be important?
- After you discuss your answers, think about the illustration and the title again. Now, what do you think the passage is about? What do you already know about this topic?

Warm-Up

Strategy: Using the Same Form of the Verb
Often an English sentence will have several verbs.

Julio Iglesias traveled to New York, performed in Radio City Music Hall, and appeared on a national television show.

Notice that all of the verbs in this sentence are in the past tense. Usually when all of the verbs in a sentence have the same subject (Julio Iglesias), they all have the same tense.

Paying attention to the verb tense in your reading will help you to know when the topic has changed. Try the following examples.

Example A

Jean enjoys watching movies and _____ about them with his friends.

talking   talk   talked

Talking is the correct answer, because it matches *watching*. Don't be confused by sentences with two subjects.

Example B

Belinda studied German and Polish, but her husband works for an Italian company so he _____ Italian every day.

studied   will study   studies

Studies is correct. The subject is *her husband*, so the answer must match *works*.

Where Have All the Young People Gone?

This reading is about changes in the lives of young and old people in a village in American Samoa. American Samoa is a territory of the United States in the southern part of the Pacific Ocean. About 27,000 people live there, and the main businesses are farming and fishing.

First try to read and understand as much of the story as you can. Then look at the Word Choices section and try to guess the missing words. Finally, you can look at the vocabulary list for help with words you don't know.

In Fiti'uta, a village in the Manu'a islands of American Samoa, there are many elderly people. When they were young, they worked in the village, _____ (1), and farmed. The men and boys spent their days working on the farms, going into the mountains to cut trees, and _____ (2) wild pigs. The women and girls took care of the children, fished, made clothing, and took care of the house.

One of the jobs of the young people was to take care of the older people in the village. They _____ (3) and carried heavy things for them and helped them in many ways. _____ (4) the people did not have very much money or possessions, they were able to take care of each other, and the older people felt comfortable.

Today, however, _____ (5) and hunting are not as important in Samoan life as they used to be. Samoans can buy their food in stores in the villages, and new houses are made of stone and metal. Cars and trucks make it fast and _____ (6) to travel around the islands. To buy all of these modern things, however, you need a lot of _____ (7), and there are few jobs in Fiti'uta that pay money. In the traditional Samoan village, people didn't need much money because they worked together cooperatively and _____ (8) the food and other things they needed.

Therefore, many young Samoans go to other places to work and make money. Some of them go to the main island of Tutuila, but there are not many jobs there either, so some go far away, to New Zealand or to the United States. Although they _____ (9) money home to their families in Fiti'uta, they cannot help the elderly people in their day-to-day lives. Many _____ (10) Samoans also go overseas to attend universities or _____ (11) professional training. It is very expensive to travel back to Samoa, so they rarely see their families in the Manu'a islands.

Now the people in Fiti'uta _____ (12) more money and can buy things they never had before, but for some of the older people, life is not as comfortable as it used to be. They wish the young people were there. They want to see them and share their life with them. Their houses are more comfortable, they can eat better food, and because of _____ (13) medicines such as penicillin, they _____ (14) longer, but they don't have very much to do. Many elderly people and young people wish the young Samoans could have good jobs but still live with their families and share _____ (15) with them in the traditional way.

Word Choices

1. fished, fishing, fish
2. hunted, hunting, will hunt
3. will cook, cooking, cooked
4. Although, Because, Since
5. farm, farming, will farm
6. easy, hard, slow
7. cooperation, time, money
8. share, shared, had shared
9. sent, send, sending
10. old, young
11. gotten, get, got
12. have, had, having
13. traditional, expensive, modern
14. lived, live, living
15. traveling, money, life

Vocabulary

elderly—old
main island—the island with the most people and biggest towns
overseas—across the ocean to other countries
possessions—things that people own
rarely—not often
traditional—the old ways, the way of life before modern times
village—a small town, usually in the country
working cooperatively—working together, sharing the work, the goals, and the reward

Comprehension Questions

1. Where is the village of Fiti'uta?
2. What did the young people used to do to help the older people?
3. In the past, why didn't the Samoans need much money?
4. Where do many young Samoans go now?
5. In what two ways is life better now for elderly Samoans?

Questions for Discussion

1. How has life in Samoa changed for young people?
2. What do you know about life on the Pacific islands? Is life on all of the islands the same?
3. What do you think will be the future of Fiti'uta and other Pacific island communities?
4. In your country, do many young people leave their homes to find jobs?
5. What do young people in your country do to help older people?
6. What can be done to help young people who want to stay in the places where they were born?

Word Choices: Correct Answers

1. fished
2. hunting
3. cooked
4. Although (There is a contrast between the two ideas, so *Although* is used.)
5. farming
6. easy
7. money (The next sentence refers to money.)
8. shared
9. send
10. young (Some older Samoans might go to a university, but the reading is about young people going away.)
11. get
12. have
13. modern (They may also use traditional medicine, but the sentence refers to penicillin, a modern drug.)
14. live
15. life ("Share life" is used earlier in the paragraph.)

Chapter 14
What Is the Definition of Peace?

Before You Read

Sit in groups of three or four. Close your eyes and picture living in peace. What are the people doing? Look at details. Are the people's lives the same as now or are they different? Are some things in your peace picture new? Are some things we have today not in your peace picture? Imagine peace for two to three minutes.

Then, open your eyes and share with the others in your group, either by speaking or writing, what you saw. Ask the others in your group questions to find out more about what they saw.

Prereading Checklist

Before you start reading the passage "What is the Definition of Peace?" skim it quickly looking for words you think might be important. Think about the illustration and the title. Try to get a general idea of what the passage is about.

Now try to answer these questions. Discuss your answers with your classmates. Thinking about these questions will help prepare you to understand and enjoy what you read.

94 / What Is the Definition of Peace?

- Does this passage mainly tell a story or does it give information?
- Is the passage about the present, the past, or the future? Or is it a combination?
- Are there people in the passage? If so, what are their names, or what else can you find out about them?
- What are some words in the passage that seem to be important?
- After you discuss your answers, think about the illustration and the title again. Now, what do you think the passage is about? What do you already know about this topic?

Warm-Up

Strategy: Using Context to Choose between Opposites
To fill in the blanks in this reading passage, you will sometimes have to choose between two words that are opposites or near opposites—for example, *happy* is the opposite of *sad*. The key to choosing the correct word is to understand the overall meaning of the reading passage.

Example A

Bruce _____ his book yesterday. Now, he has to buy a new one.

found   lost

Lost is the correct choice because the next sentence tells us that Bruce needs a new book. Often when we lose something we need to buy a new one.

Example B

Tom _____ his wife. Every time he sees her, he has a big smile on his face.

hates   loves

Loves is the correct choice. Usually, we do not smile when we see someone we hate.

Example C

Arnold and Josefina argued and fought for years. Finally, they decided to get _____ .

divorced   married

Divorced is probably the correct choice. Although some couples seem to love to fight, most people don't want to marry someone with whom they argue and fight.

What Is the Definition of Peace?

Sometimes it seems that there is not much peace in the world. Fortunately, people in many countries are working to bring about peace. This reading passage talks about what peace means. First, try to read and understand as much of the passage as you can. Then look at the Word Choices section and try to guess the missing words. Finally, you can look at the vocabulary list for help with words you don't know.

People use opposites to understand ideas. For example, what is happiness? It is the opposite of sadness. What is old? It is the opposite of _____ (1). People also use opposites to think about the definition of peace. We often say that peace is the opposite of war.

However, there _____ (2) to define peace. Some people say that peace means more than "no war." Every year, many people die in wars, but many more people are _____ (3) in other ways.

Each year millions of children and adults die because they do not have enough food. There is enough food in the world to feed everyone, _____ (4) some people never get the food they need. These hungry people do not have enough money to _____ (5) the food they need. These people are not fighting in a war, but they do not have peace in their life either. Therefore, maybe peace is also the opposite of hunger.

Another cause of death for millions of people every year _____ (6) disease. Many killer diseases can be _____ (7) by clean water or cured by medicine. Dysentery is a disease that can be prevented. _____ (8) people die of dysentery in developed countries, such as the United Sates, but many people in poor countries die of dysentery and other preventable diseases. Therefore, maybe peace is _____ (9) the opposite of preventable disease.

There are many wars between countries. However, people also are killed by people from _____ (10) own country. One way this happens is when the government kills its own people.

_____ (11), in some countries throughout the world, the people say that they do not have freedom. They say that when they try to change their society to get more freedom, the _____ (12) puts them in jail or kills them. Therefore, maybe peace is also the opposite of government killing.

_____ (13) wants to have peace in the world. What is the definition of peace? _____ (14), it is the opposite of war, but it can also be more. Peace can also mean that everyone has enough to eat, _____ (15) water, medicine, and that governments do not kill their own people.

Word Choices

1. elderly, young
2. are many ways, is only one way
3. born, killed
4. because, but, so
5. buy, sell
6. are, is
7. caused, prevented
8. Few, Many
9. also, not
10. her, his, their
11. Also, For example, Therefore
12. disease, freedom, government
13. Everyone, No one
14. No, Yes
15. clean, dirty

Vocabulary

cured—brought back to good health, made well

developed countries—rich, industrial countries

dysentery—a disease caused by drinking dirty water

jail—a place where police put people, a place that you cannot leave unless the police let you leave

Comprehension Questions

1. Are more people killed in wars, or are more people killed in other ways?
2. Is there enough food in the world to feed everyone?
3. Do many people in the United States die of dysentery? Where is dysentery a problem?
4. What can be done to prevent and cure many killer diseases?
5. How can people be killed when they are not in a war?

Questions for Discussion

1. In the reading passage, there are two definitions of peace. One says that peace is the opposite of war. The other definition says that peace is also the opposite of hunger, preventable disease, etc. Which definition do you agree with?

2. Can you think of a country where the government is killing its own people? What do you know about that country?
3. What other preventable diseases do you know about? How can they be prevented?
4. How can understanding the meaning of peace help us achieve peace?
5. Twenty years from now, do you think there will be more peace in the world or less?

Word Choices: Correct Answers

1. young
2. are many ways (The main idea of the reading passage is that there is *more than one* way to define peace.)
3. killed (The passage is about how people are killed, not about how they are born.)
4. but (There is a *contrast* between "there is enough food in the world to feed everyone" and "some people never get the food they need.")
5. buy (Money is needed to *buy* food.)
6. is (The subject of the sentence is *reason*.)
7. prevented
8. Few (In the sentence *but* shows there is contrast. The contrast is between *many* people dying of dysentery in developing countries and *few* people dying of dysentery in the United States.)
9. also
10. their
11. For example
12. government
13. Everyone
14. Yes
15. clean (Clean water helps people live. Dirty water carries disease.)

Answers to Comprehension Questions

A Note to the Teacher

The comprehension questions are designed to assure that the students understood the general idea of each reading. They are not designed to be used as a test. The answers below are a guideline. Listen carefully to the students' answers. Sometimes even when they give a different answer you can see that they generally understood the reading but missed a particular point. This is a good time to help them with their reading strategies. Don't worry too much about their grammar or about their making complete sentences as they give their answers. They should be concentrating on *understanding,* not on responding with perfect grammar.

Chapter 1: Going to School in Other Countries

1. Meiji Gakuin is in the United States of America.
2. The Canadian Academy is in Kobe, Japan.
3. No, they could not live in the foreigners' section.
4. They want their children to study in their own language and to learn the same things that children in their home country are learning.
5. They believe that learning about the people, the language, and the culture of the foreign country is an important part of living overseas.

Chapter 2: How Long Will You Live?

1. People live longer today.
2. Only 80 percent of babies lived to be one year old.
3. There are more widows, because many women in Japan live longer than their husbands.
4. Thousands of people die each year in wars.
5. Two reasons are that people drink cleaner water and the medicine is better.

Chapter 3: From the Village to the City

1. Mexico City is very different now. There are many more people, it is busier and noisier, and Mrs. Sandoval thinks that people are not as friendly as they used to be.
2. They come to find jobs and to have electricity, public transportation, and other features of modern city life.
3. Maria was born in Mexico City.
4. Mrs. Sandoval was born in a village.
5. She prefers to live in the city because it is more comfortable.

Chapter 4: A New Future

1. A stranger came to Pomeray.
2. They were excited about his offer. They thought they would become rich.
3. No, not everyone agreed.
4. They did not become rich. Other people came and got the good jobs. The towns became larger and the people could not control the change.
5. They worked with the factory owner to make a plan for the future. After they had planned, they agreed to build the factory.

Chapter 5: Guns, Guns, Too Many Guns?

1. Gun control is one of the biggest issues.
2. No, some countries do not allow people to buy pistols or rifles.
3. They want guns for hunting and for their safety. Some people also use guns for target practice.
4. Only the police and the military could still have guns.
5. Martin Luther King, Jr., and John Kennedy, among others.

Chapter 6: Two Kinds of Medicine

1. His back hurts.
2. No, he doesn't.
3. No, because it doesn't taste good.
4. Long ago, traditional medicine was much more popular.
5. People in England use modern medicine. Only a few people there know about traditional medicine.
6. Traditional Chinese medicine is in the ball.

Chapter 7: Learning about Other Countries without Leaving Home

1. Jerry was a farmer.
2. Jerry didn't go to college. He stayed to help his father on the farm.
3. He met them in the United States.
4. They were poor, did not speak English, and did not know about life in the United States.
5. They had both language and cultural differences at first.

Chapter 8: Is There Enough Food in the World for Everyone?

1. Hunger makes people weak, and weak people die easily of disease.
2. Yes, there is enough food in the world to feed everyone.
3. It is true.
4. The countries need money to buy imports, and the hungry people in that country do not have enough money to buy the food.
5. The companies must sell the food to pay their workers and have a successful business.

Chapter 9: Two Friends with Different Futures

1. They are Native Americans who live in many parts of the state of Alaska.
2. Elena was born in Fairbanks, Alaska, and Shelly was born in a small town in the country.
3. Shelly could speak Yup'ik better because she lived in a town were everybody used Yup'ik every day.
4. Elena wanted to teach for a short time, then work in her own business. Shelly wanted to go back to her village and teach.
5. She could speak both Yup'ik and English, so she could teach them about their native culture and the modern world.

Chapter 10: Clean Water and the Women of Burkina Faso

1. Thirty percent of the earth is covered by land.
2. The UN wanted everyone to have clean water, and they wanted everyone to be able to get water easily.
3. The women usually do this job.
4. They built a dam.
5. First it rained, then the people had a celebration.

Chapter 11: Can the Rain Forests Be Saved?

1. The Amazon river is nearly 6,500 kilometers (4,000 miles) long.
2. Because of the heavy rain that falls there.
3. No. It started about four hundred years ago, but has become a major problem only recently.
4. The rainclouds over the Amazon block some of the sunlight and keep the earth cool. If they disappear, the earth will become warmer.
5. He was killed for fighting against the clearing of the forest.

Chapter 12: Are Languages Alive?

1. A dead language is a language that stops changing.
2. *Spacey* and *dropout* are now used by almost everybody.
3. *Pasokon* is a new Japanese word that means "personal computer."
4. Many English words come from Latin, German, and French.
5. No. When people use a language, it changes.

Chapter 13: Where Have All the Young People Gone?

1. Fiti'uta is in the islands of Manu'a in American Samoa. American Samoa is in the south Pacific Ocean.
2. Among other things, they cooked for them and carried heavy things.
3. They didn't need money because everybody in the village worked together and shared what they had. They need money now to buy modern things that they cannot make.
4. Many of them leave the village and go to the main island or go overseas to find jobs.
5. They have more money, and they live longer. They also have better food.

Chapter 14: What Is the Definition of Peace?

1. More people are killed in other ways besides war.
2. Yes, but still some people do not get the food they need.
3. No. Dysentery is a problem in poor countries with dirty water.
4. Clean water can help prevent some diseases, and medicine can cure some diseases.
5. People can be killed by hunger, by disease, or by their own government.